WITHDRAWN

We Want to Go to School!

The Fight for Disability Rights

by
Maryann Cocca-Leffler
& Janine Leffler

Albert Whitman & Company
Chicago, Illinois

"In these days, it is doubtful that any child may reasonably be expected to succeed in life if he is denied the opportunity of an education."

—Chief Justice Earl Warren,
Brown v. Board of Education, 1954

To public schools everywhere who open their doors to all,
and to the educators who open their hearts.
Thank you.—MCL & JL

Library of Congress Cataloging-in-Publication data is on file with the publisher.
Text and illustrations copyright © 2021 by Maryann Cocca-Leffler
First published in the United States of America in 2021 by Albert Whitman & Company
ISBN 978-0-8075-3518-9 (hardcover)
ISBN 978-0-8075-3515-8 (ebook)

Printed in China
10 9 8 7 6 5 4 3 2 1 RRD 26 25 24 23 22 21

Design by Rick DeMonico

For more information about Albert Whitman & Company,
visit our website at www.albertwhitman.com.

Hi, I'm Janine.

When I was a kid, it took me a long time to learn
to talk and walk.

My muscles were weak.

I was born with something called cerebral palsy,
or CP for short.

I learned to read before I could talk,
but I needed help doing lots of other things.

So when I was three years old, I took a bus every day to a public school in my town.

I had lots of teachers.

I had a classroom teacher,

a teacher to help me
build my muscles,

Physical
Therapist

Speech
Therapist

a teacher to help me
learn to talk,

Occupational
Therapist

and a
teacher to
help me
use my
hands.

From one school year to the next, I learned side by side with my friends.

Together we...

laughed,

played,

studied,

worked on projects,

and cheered.

I needed help along the way and extra time to get things done, but I was always part of the class.

It is the same way for other kids
with disabilities all around America.

But one day I read that it hadn't always been that way…

In the early 1970s, millions of children with disabilities weren't allowed to go to public schools.

Most of the time, they stayed at home or lived in hospitals, where they didn't learn much of anything. Or their families had to pay to send them to special schools.

Sometimes, children with disabilities were allowed to take tests to try to get into a public school. But if they got in, they were placed in segregated classrooms, away from everyone and everything, and not given the same quality of education as the other kids.

Public schools everywhere said NO to millions of children who wanted to go to school.

But in 1971 in Washington, DC, seven school-age children were tired of hearing NO!

They wanted to go to school too.

George Liddell, Jr.

Steven Gaston

Duane Blacksheare

They all had disabilities, and none of them were allowed to go to public school.

It didn't feel good to be left out.

The kids and their families asked,

Why?

The children and their families made their voices heard.

The schools weren't listening, and the families were getting mad.

Many of these parents grew up in the 1950s, when they were the students who were being segregated. Only back then it was because of the color of their skin.

Now it was 1971, and their children were not allowed to go to public school because of their disabilities.

But I want to go to school.

The parents thought about the *Brown v. Board of Education* case from 1954, when the Supreme Court decided that every child has a right to get an equal education. Their children were not getting an equal education...and in most cases, they weren't getting any education at all!

What about equal education for OUR children?

THE TOPEKA

STATE JOURNAL

MONDAY · MAY 17, 1954

Home Edition
FIVE CENTS

SCHOOL SEGREGATION BANNED

Supreme Court Refutes Doctrine of Separate but Equal Education

The children and their families began meeting.

They decided to join together and file a lawsuit against the school district.

It was time to fight for their rights!

Four lawyers took the case. It was called *Mills v. Board of Education of the District of Columbia*. The case was named after one of the seven children, Peter Mills, a twelve-year-old boy with disabilities.

Soon, word started to spread. More families joined the lawsuit.

It was a *class action suit*, which meant that it stood up for a lot of children. And I mean a LOT!

18,000 students from the Washington, DC, area were also not receiving a public education because of their disabilities.

18,000. Try to imagine 18,000.

Then try to imagine 8,000,000 (8 million)!
That's how many children in the
United States weren't getting an education
because they had disabilities.

On September 24, 1971, the case, *Mills v. Board of Education*, was filed in the United States District Court for the District of Columbia. Judge Joseph C. Waddy would decide the case.

The lawyers for the children fought hard:

All students are equal, and by not letting children with disabilities attend public school, the school is taking away their rights.

In *Brown v. Board of Education*, it was decided that children have the right to a free, equal public education no matter their race. I argue that this right is for all children, regardless of their race, gender, or disability.

The lawyers for the schools argued:

The schools can't possibly afford to pay for the education of these children.

Judge Waddy listened to both sides.

There were lots of delays.

It took a while for Judge Waddy to make his final judgment. He thought and thought...

On one hand, he knew that it would cost the schools a lot of money to provide an education to these children.

On the other hand, shouldn't schools be spending their money on ALL children?

Finally, on August 1, 1972, Judge Joseph C. Waddy was ready to announce his decision.

The kids wondered…would they finally be able to go to school with everyone else?

The families wondered…would their children finally be included?

Yes! They Won!

The court ruled that students with disabilities must be given a free public education.

That fall, all across Washington, DC, thousands of kids were now able to go to school with their friends.

It didn't end there.
Actually, it was just the beginning.

Mills v. Board of Education inspired more federal court cases, leading to important federal laws guaranteeing public education for all children.

All across the country, millions of students with disabilities could finally go to school and get the education they needed and deserved.

Thank you, Peter, Janice, Jerome, Michael, George, Steven, and Duane.

You changed many lives... including mine.

About Disability Education Rights in the United States

For many years, children with disabilities in the United States were legally excluded from public schools. Unless their families could afford to send them to private schools, these children remained in institutions, hospitals, or at home. Children with mild disabilities were sometimes allowed to attend public school, only to be segregated from their peers and given inadequate educations. School administrators argued that children with disabilities were unable to learn, would distract the other students, and required too much time and money.

Of course, children with disabilities *can* learn. And so the families and guardians of seven children with disabilities living in Washington, DC, joined together to fight for the right to go to school. In September 1971, they filed a lawsuit against the Board of Education of the District of Columbia in US district court. The case was called *Mills v. Board of Education of the District of Columbia*, named after one of the plaintiffs, a boy named Peter Mills. It was a class action suit, representing not only these seven children, but more than 18,000 students in the Washington, DC, area excluded from public education because of their disabilities. The case was heard by Judge Joseph Cornelius Waddy, one of the first Black judges to be appointed to a federal district court bench.

Mills wasn't the only lawsuit of its kind at the time. Another case, *Pennsylvania Association of Retarded Citizens (PARC) v. Commonwealth of Pennsylvania*, was filed by families of children with cognitive disabilities who were kept out of public school. But the *Mills v. Board of Education* case went further by representing children with a variety of disabilities, including physical, emotional, developmental, and behavioral issues.

The *Mills* lawyers cited the 1954 landmark civil rights case *Brown v. Board of Education* as precedent. Though the *Brown* case addressed racial segregation, its decision led to a growing understanding that all people—regardless of race, gender, or disability—have the right to a public education.

On August 1, 1972, after giving the school board time to formulate comprehensive plans, with no results, Judge Waddy finally made his decision on the *Mills* case:

> The District of Columbia shall provide to each child of school age a free and suitable publicly supported education regardless of the degree of the child's mental, physical, or emotional disability or impairment. Furthermore, defendants shall not exclude any child resident in the District of Columbia from such publicly supported education on the basis of a claim of insufficient resources.

That year, children with disabilities in Washington, DC, began going to public school, side by side with everyone else.

The *Mills* and the *PARC* cases were catalysts for change. In 1975 the Education for All Handicapped Children Act (EAHCA) was created, and with it the Individualized Education Plan (IEP), in which parents and educators work together to determine each child's goals. Over the years, this act, later called the Individuals with Disabilities Education Act (IDEA), has been amended and improved to ensure that students with disabilities continue to receive a free, appropriate, public education.

Timeline

1954 **The *Brown v. Board of Education* case** is decided by the US Supreme Court, which rules that racial segregation in public schools is unconstitutional.

1972 In ***PARC v. Commonwealth of Pennsylvania*** and ***Mills v. Board of Education***, two US District Courts rule that children with disabilities have the right to a free public education.

1973 **The Rehabilitation Act of 1973** prohibits federal agencies from discriminating against people with disabilities, though some proposed amendments do not become laws until years later.

1975 President Ford signs the **Education for All Handicapped Children Act (EAHCA)**, stating that all children with disabilities have the right to a free, appropriate, public education.

1977 On April 5, more than one hundred demonstrators with disabilities take over a federal building in San Francisco, beginning the **504 Sit-In** to protest the delays in signing Section 504 of the Rehabilitation Act of 1973, a law requiring government facilities, including schools and state colleges and universities, to be accessible for people with disabilities. At last, on April 28, Section 504 is signed into law and the sit-in ends a few days later.

1990 **The Americans with Disabilities Act (ADA)** is signed by President George H. W. Bush, prohibiting discrimination against individuals with disabilities in all areas of public life, ensuring they have the same rights and opportunities as everyone else. The **EAHCA** is renamed the **Individuals with Disabilities Education Act (IDEA)**.

2004 Congress amends **IDEA** to ensure children with disabilities are better prepared for further education, employment, and independent living.

2014 President Obama signs **Section 503 of the Rehabilitation Act of 1973**, which requires employers who receive federal funds to take affirmative action to recruit, hire, and promote individuals with disabilities.

A Note from Janine

In 1985 I was born with cerebral palsy, which affected my muscles, vision, and cognitive abilities. Throughout my fifteen years in public school, I learned side by side with my classmates. I thrived because of the interactions I had with my peers and made many friends. I received the therapies and accommodations I needed to succeed in school and go on to college, where I earned my BA. I am grateful to those students and families who stood up for OUR right to attend public school in 1971.

I often get asked, if I could snap my fingers and not have any disabilities, would I? There is only one answer: NO. I will never drive, ride a bike, or tie my shoes, but my challenges made me who I am today. It is the inside that counts. I focus on what I can do—not what I cannot do—and continue to live my best life. I hope you do too.

A Note from Maryann

As I researched this book, my heart ached. I cannot imagine the pain, helplessness, and discrimination that these families felt when their children were denied an education. We owe them a debt of gratitude. I have been an advocate for my daughter Janine from day one and have guided her through public school and beyond. I cannot imagine Janine's life without the support of the public schools and the dedicated teachers and therapists. Of course, there were a few bumps along the way as the schools and I decided on the best learning approach for Janine. I realize now that *my* right as a parent to voice my views and guide her Individualized Education Plan (IEP) was also the result of changes brought about by cases like *Mills*, a right that didn't exist prior to 1975.

I am also thankful to Judge Joseph C. Waddy for his brave ruling and to the legal team who took on the *Mills* case. I was very fortunate to connect with the last surviving lawyer, Paul R. Dimond, who graciously gave me firsthand insight into this landmark case, which continues to impact the lives of many students throughout their school years.

But the biggest challenge for students with disabilities may lie beyond school, when they seek employment after age twenty-one. Unfortunately, the majority of adults with intellectual and developmental disabilities are either unemployed or underemployed, despite their ability, desire, and willingness to work. Society has the responsibility to ensure that every person is included in the workplace and in all walks of life with respect and acceptance. Let's work together to continue to support the rights of the disabled community by upholding and strengthening the laws.